YOUNGEST RECRUITS

Youngest Recruits

Pre-War, War & Post-War Experiences
in Western Côte d'Ivoire

Magali Chelpi-den Hamer

PALLAS PUBLICATIONS

Cover illustration: Paul Dehédin
Cover design: Maedium, Utrecht
Lay out: V3-Services, Baarn

ISBN   978 90 8555 028 0
e-ISBN   978 90 4851 173 0
NUR   740

© M. Chelpi-den Hamer / Pallas Publications – Amsterdam University Press 2010

All rights reserved. Without limiting the rights under copyright reserved above, no part of this book may be reproduced, stored in or introduced into a retrieval system, or transmitted, in any form or by any means (electronic, mechanical, photocopying, recording or otherwise) without the written permission of both the copyright owner and the author of the book.

Table of contents

Acknowledgements 7
List of Acronyms 9
Introduction 11

1 **Contextual Information & Particularities of the Ivoirian Case** 13
   1.1 Children's Demobilisation from the Rebel Side 13
   1.2 Children's Demobilisation from Pro-Governmental Militias 15
   1.3 Particularities of the Ivoirian Case 16

2 **Research Approach** 19
   2.1 Description of the Sample & Research Approach 19
   2.2 Prevention, Demobilisation and Reintegration Programming 20

3 **Pre-War Trajectories** 23
   3.1 Educational Trajectories 23
   3.2 Professional Trajectories 25
   3.3 Relationships with the Family / Social Connectedness 28

4 **Wartime Experiences** 31
   4.1 Motivations to Join 31
   4.2 Actions in Warfare 34

5 **Post-War Trajectories** 39
   5.1 Demobilisation 39
   5.2 Social Reinsertion 42
   5.3 Going Back to School? 45
   5.4 Reinserting Through and Outside Projects 46

6   Concluding Remarks & Reflections on Child Soldiering   49
   6.1   Reflections on Child Soldiering   50

Notes   57
References   61

APPENDIX: Interview Guide (in French) – Checklist   65

Acknowledgements

Collecting primary information is always challenging, and this work could not have been written without the contribution of key partners. I would like to take this opportunity to thank them all. I am especially grateful to the local NGO ODAFEM, which facilitated my access to the care centre they were running. Many thanks also to the International Rescue Committee, which hosted me during that period and continues to follow some of the young people I interviewed through their child protection and development program. Special thanks go to the boys and girls who unconditionally agreed to share with me their difficult personal stories. Their experiences are extraordinary. I tried my best to give them all the credit they deserve. If I distorted any meaning in the process, I sincerely apologise.

Many thanks to Paul Dehédin, who was kind enough to allow me to use one of his drawings for the cover page, and to David Raats who was the first to correct my imperfect English.

Part of the financing for the writing and publication of this booklet has been generously provided by the International Rescue Committee with support from Stichting Vluchteling. Stichting Vluchteling used funds from the Dutch Postcode Lottery to subsidise this project.

The views and opinions expressed in this monograph are those of the author and do not necessarily represent the views of any of the institutions previously cited.

List of Acronyms

APWé	Patriotic Alliance of Wé (pro-governmental militia)
CTO	Orientation and Transit Centre
DDR	Disarmament, Demobilisation and Reinsertion
Etat Major	(French term) Military leadership
FAFN	Armed Forces of the Forces Nouvelles (rebel forces)
FANCI / FDS	National Armed Forces of Côte d'Ivoire (government forces)
FLGO	Front for the Liberation of the Great West (pro-governmental militia)
IRC	International Rescue Committee
LRA	Lord Resistance Army
MILOCI	Ivoirian Movement for the Liberation of the West of Côte d'Ivoire (pro-governmental militia)
ONUCI	UN Operation in Côte d'Ivoire
PDR	Prevention, Demobilisation and Reintegration programming
PNDDR	National Program of Disarmament, Demobilisation and Reinsertion
RUF	Revolutionary Unitary Front
UNICEF	United Nations Children's Fund
UPRGO	Union of Patriots for the Resistance of the Great West (pro-governmental militia)
WFP	World Food Program

Introduction

The participation of children and adolescents in violent conflicts is the gloomy reality of many wars, and Côte d'Ivoire is no exception. Despite a lack of empirical evidence, it is often assumed that they follow different patterns of mobilisation than their older peers, and much of the literature on children's involvement in military action emphasises their limited agency when they enlist in violent groups. Cases of abduction have received a lot of media coverage in recent years, with stories of youths coerced into violent movements such as the LRA or the RUF, and there has been a proliferation of articles and reports documenting such practices. If most of these failed to engage in key debates, they did have a major impact in shaping the dominant discourse and international public opinion on child soldiering, with the main pitfall being the oversimplification of children's motives for engagement by reducing the issue to forced conscription and manipulable minds. Conversely, ethnographic studies have highlighted the complexity of the processes of mobilisation of children and adolescents, by recognising their multiplicity of patterns and by acknowledging some similarities with processes of mobilisation of the older generation.

This booklet explores the profiles and motives that made children and adolescents enlist into an armed group during the Ivoirian conflict. Its objective is to raise public awareness of the complexity of child soldiering and to point out the multiplicity of patterns. It is intended for anyone interested in this theme, from practitioners to any individuals wishing to understand the nature and scope of this phenomenon a bit more by looking at data recently collected in Côte d'Ivoire. The booklet addresses a number of questions: among the very youngest, are there certain personal profiles more likely to become involved in violent groups? Do they share some similarities with the older recruits? Do they exhibit different post-war trajectories? Despite many set ideas on who joins armed groups and why, these remain empirical questions whose answers vary considerably across contexts.

Chapter 1 presents some contextual information, discusses children's processes of demobilisation in both rebel and pro-governmental militias, and points out some particularities of the Ivoirian case. Chapter 2 explains the research approach. Chapters 3, 4 and 5 explore the pre-war, wartime, and post-war trajectories of the youngest recruits. Chapter 6 reflects on some of the current debates associated with child soldiering and offers some recommendations, based on this case study. The bulk of the data is based on in-depth interviews with demobilised child soldiers in the rebel stronghold of Man, western Côte d'Ivoire, an area severely affected by the Ivoirian conflict.

1 Contextual Information & Particularities of the Ivoirian Case

Côte d'Ivoire has been split into two since September 2002. Rebel forces are in control of the northern part of the country and the main towns of Bouaké, Korhogo and Man, while the southern part has stayed under government control, including the towns of Abidjan, Yamoussoukro, Daloa, and all the ports in the coastal area. There has recently been some progress in the redeployment of the state administration in the North. However, many challenges remain, and *de facto*, the rebellion is still administrating key sectors in its zone.

In terms of child soldiering, both rebel and pro-governmental militias have officially acknowledged that they had some under-eighteens in their troops in the beginning of the war.[1] At the same time, they strongly denied having consciously recruited them. They have, however, shown a relative openness towards putting an end to the practice. The use of children as soldiers has come to be perceived so negatively in recent years, especially on the international scene, that parties to conflicts generally tend to be rather cooperative about stopping the practice, once the conflict has peaked. I describe below the main steps taken by the belligerents to ensure children's demobilisation from their ranks, while highlighting some particularities of the Ivoirian case.

1.1 Children's Demobilisation from the Rebel Side

Following the signing of a comprehensive cease-fire between the national army (FANCI) and the rebel forces (FAFN)[2] and the joint end-of-war declaration,[3] UNICEF established direct dialogue with the main belligerents in order to raise their awareness of child soldiering. This resulted in an official declaration by FAFN officials on 15 September 2003 stating that the rebellion would put an end to the recruitment of children into its ranks; it also announced the release of 273 child soldiers (United Nations, 2005).

Since that declaration, the peace process has stalled several times, which mainly resulted in delaying the demobilisation process of the youngest recruits. In matters of child soldiering, belligerents only resumed a dialogue after the adoption of UN resolution 1612 in July 2005. In August of the same year, ONUCI child protection representatives held a meeting with FAFN commanders in Bouaké, during which they pointed out that the continuing use of child soldiers in the rebel ranks had prompted the inclusion of FAFN on the list of violators in the 2005 report on Children and Armed Conflict, addressed to the UN Security Council. Consequently, the UN Security Council requested the preparation and implementation without delay of an action plan to halt the recruitment and use of child soldiers in Côte d'Ivoire.

UN representatives in Côte d'Ivoire therefore drafted a plan that called on all armed groups to cease recruiting children and to collaborate with UNICEF for the identification and reintegration of children still in the military camps. Three months later,[4] FAFN leadership approved and signed the plan, and submitted it to the UN Secretary-General Special Representative in Côte d'Ivoire. They specifically committed to end the use of child soldiers, to release all children in their ranks, to carry out specific measures to prevent the recruitment of children – including the issuing of formal instructions through their chain of command – and to cooperate with the national disarmament, demobilisation and reintegration programme on children's issues.[5] In order to smooth the implementation of the plan, UNICEF and FAFN also agreed on the following points: 1) in each of the ten areas under FAFN control, the set-up of a focal point for the monitoring of Prevention, Demobilisation and Reinsertion activities (PDR); 2) the training of focal point staff by UNICEF and child protection agencies in international humanitarian law, child protection issues and the provisions of UN Security Council Resolutions; 3) the signing of a performance contract describing the activities to be undertaken (identification, demobilisation, awareness-raising with camp leaders) and the exact time frame for implementation with each focal point; and 4) the establishing of a verification committee comprising non-governmental actors involved in PDR activities (International Rescue Committee, Save the Children UK, and Save the Children Sweden) to carry out unannounced visits to military camps.[6]

UN monitoring and verification teams confirmed that no children had enlisted on the rebel side in 2005 and 2006, and that measures were taken by the rebel leadership to identify children enrolled before 2005, so that they could be handed over to child protection staff. In 2005, 327 children were officially demobilised in FAFN-controlled areas, 251 of whom were physically handed over to UN staff (United Nations, 2006b). In the same period, UNICEF reported the self-demobilisation of 600 children in Danané who had been recruited by pro-rebel Liberian mercenaries. On 1 July 2006, FAFN leadership submitted a follow-up report to the UN Secretary-General Special Representative in Côte d'Ivoire, stating that there were no more children associated with their fighting forces in the military zones of Bouaké and Katiola. In the remaining eight zones under their control, they were still pursuing efforts to identify child soldiers and hand them over to UNICEF, but reported anticipating difficulties due to strained resources (United Nations, 2006b).

At the end of 2006, ONUCI child protection representatives met again with FAFN leaders to present and discuss the annual report on Children and Armed Conflict in Côte d'Ivoire, addressed to the UN Security Council. FAFN objected to the continued inclusion of their movement in the list of the violating parties, arguing that they had made substantive efforts to stop the association of children with their forces. They also reiterated their position of not having a recruiting policy for children. If children were found around FAFN military camps, the official position was that they were merely interacting with FAFN recruits in order to get some kind of minor assistance.

FAFN leadership submitted a letter to UNICEF in early 2007 requesting material support in order to fully implement the action plan submitted to the United Nations. In mid-March of the same year, an agreement was signed between UNICEF and the National Program of Disarmament, Demobilisation and Reinsertion (PNDDR), whereby UNICEF committed to provide logistical support to FAFN to facilitate the identification and demobilisation of all children in their ranks. In June, FAFN child protection focal points received an in-kind donation of ten motorcycles to enable them to travel to the different military zones for the identification and demobilisation of the remaining children. At the end of the summer of 2007, FAFN reported having demobilised 85 children, including 27 girls (United Nations, 2007).

1.2 Children's Demobilisation from Pro-Governmental Militias

A similar approach was adopted for the FANCI and pro-governmental militias. During a seminar in Grand Bassam on 5 and 6 October 2003, UNICEF explained to the regular army why children should not be associated with armed activities, why a separate process was required for their demobilisation and reinsertion, and what the UNICEF Prevention, Demobilisation and Reinsertion activities were. To date, there is no tangible evidence of children having enlisted into FANCI's ranks. However, at the peak of the conflict, the links between FANCI and pro-governmental militias were so blurred that this fear cannot in all certainty be discarded.

With the pro-governmental militias, lack of clarity in their chains of command had made it difficult to make any substantial progress quickly. While the rebel leadership had submitted a comprehensive action plan to the Security Council at the end of 2005, it took another year for militia leaders to do the same. Finally, at the end of 2006, continuous lobbying from ONUCI, UNICEF, PNDDR and child protection agencies bore fruit and led the four main militia leaders[7] to submit an action plan to the UN Secretary-General Special Representative in Côte d'Ivoire,[8] showing their commitment to end the use of children in their ranks and to release 100 children associated with their forces. These children were the first to be officially demobilised.[9] Eleven other children were screened out later in 2006, out of the 981 militia recruits who had undergone the official process of demobilisation in the summer of the same year.[10]

In April 2007, militia focal points began a process of identification of children associated with their forces in Guiglo, Toulépleu, Blolequin, Tai, Zagné, Duékoué and Bangolo. This ten-day exercise led to the registration of 204 children, including 84 girls. Most of these were handed over shortly afterwards to UNICEF and child protection agencies in order to receive reinsertion assistance.

1.3 Particularities of the Ivoirian Case

In addition to the general debates associated with child soldiering upon which I reflect in the last chapter (their degree of agency in warfare, the relevance of separate treatments for child and adult demobilised recruits, how to address stigma), there are a number of particularities to take into account in the Ivoirian case.

First, while some children were still based in military camps when they were demobilised, others had already dispersed and were already reunified with their families and communities. In line with the UN guidelines on how to handle such youths – 'Children who have already found their way back home to their families and communities should under no circumstances be removed in order to enter cantonment sites and join a formal demobilisation process' (United Nations, 2006a) – we would have expected external interventions to focus on community-wide reinsertion programs from the start, to provide the least disruption of these children's lives. Conversely, the bulk of the demobilised children entered transitional care centres after being identified as former recruits and were cut off from their direct environment for several weeks, even those who had already returned home years ago.[11]

The second particularity to take into account is that, in 2005-2006, the standard intervention was still to use boarding care centres as the main reinsertion tools, regardless of individual situations. In Man, my fieldwork location, such an approach was consolidated in February 2005 with the start of UNICEF-funded PDR activities, exclusively benefitting children associated with armed forces who were hosted in two nearby transition centres (CTO). Over the years, PDR activities evolved, and child protection agencies started to use community-wide approaches, moving beyond PDR activities that only benefited children associated with armed groups, to the supply of psychological and reinsertion assistance on site to broadly defined 'war-affected' populations. Such a shift in practice has been remarkable since 2006 and marks an important step in the international response to child soldiering.

A third particularity, surely not confined to the Ivoirian case, is that many of the interviewed children demobilised outside an existing framework. Some fled their group when an opportunity arose, while others were discharged by their chiefs months or years after they joined, without receiving compensation for services rendered. Some of these self-demobilised children were traced by child protection agencies. In 2005-2006, in war-affected areas, local and international NGOs toured villages, particularly in zones that had seen violence, and approached village chiefs and other prominent local inhabitants with the tentative aim of identifying children who had participated in warfare, in order to provide them with some *a posteriori* reinsertion assistance.[12]

Fourth, the myth of the regional warrior is firmly anchored in West Africa and has been reinforced by the extremely violent conflict experiences in Liberia and Sierra Leone. Social workers working with demobilised children in Liberia reported that many of them had been re-recruited to fight in the Ivoirian conflict, especially in counties bordering Côte d'Ivoire (Human Rights Watch, 2005). The Ivoirian government's raids on the main rebel-held cities of Bouaké and Korhogo in November 2004 undoubtedly spawned an increase in recruitment; however, there is still a lack of empirical evidence to be able to capture the scale and complexity of these cross-border processes of mobilisation.

The final point I want to make relates to the opaque nature of numbers. There is little hope of getting a good approximation of the number of child recruits in the Ivoirian conflict, let alone the number of those who did not enter formal demobilisation and reinsertion. Numbers used by the UN are based on FAFN and militia lists and are only reported cases of demobilisation or rule-of-thumb figures, which say little about the scope of the phenomenon.[13] Intuitively, one could argue that child recruitment in Côte d'Ivoire was not as massive in scale as during the Liberian and Sierra Leone wars. The conflict did not last long, and the main period of violence only lasted a few months in the West, from the end of 2002 to mid-spring 2003, with a short peak in November 2004. This is not to suggest that extreme violence was absent in the Ivoirian war. Liberian mercenaries, in both rebel and pro-governmental forces, were in fact particularly prone to committing the most barbaric acts on civilians.

2 Research Approach

The empirical data is based on 21 semi-structured interviews with boys and girls formerly enrolled in armed groups and involved in an NGO-led reinsertion project.[14] The bulk of the data was collected in Man, a major rebel stronghold in western Côte d'Ivoire, in December 2006 and June 2007, and was supplemented by the analysis of 32 other profiles compiled by the NGO. Of the 21 children directly interviewed by the author, follow-up interviews were done with 14 children in December 2007 to get a sense of how they were getting on a year later, of which 10, who are now adults, continue to be followed by the author.

2.1 Description of the Sample & Research Approach

At the time of the interviews, respondents were between 14 and 18 years old. This was approximately three or four years after their enlistment into an armed group, which means that they were between 10 and 14 years old when they were recruited. This is well below the acceptable age in Côte d'Ivoire, even if we take the pragmatic view of tolerating recruitment into armed groups for the oldest teenagers. The profiles compiled by the NGO included some young adults up to 22 years old, who were around 18 when they joined the rebel forces.

The youths I met usually carried a towel carelessly thrown over their shoulder. I remember thinking this was an amusing detail, especially since they seemed to pass the same towel to each other each time I started a discussion with someone new. Interviews were done in the transition centre that was hosting these children, either inside, in a quiet room, or outside, facing each other or sitting on some steps with no one around. Our dialogues were filmed, unless the children did not consent, which never happened. I forgot my camera twice during the period I did interviews, and each time, the children expressed some disappointment. During my first visit to the centre, the staff organised an informal meeting with all the children, where I took the time to introduce myself and to explain that I was interested in hearing their life stories to compile them in a book. I emphasised that I was not interested in names, but in understanding how and why they had ended up the way they had. I wanted to talk about their pre-war lives (education, work – if any, relationships with family, social networks), their actions during the war (mainly, whatever they wanted to tell me about that period and their interpretation of their enlistment), and how they saw their future and their options outside armed groups (including what their views were on the reinsertion project). I also re-emphasised that interviews were not compulsory and that nobody had to meet with me if they did not want to. I stressed that I was not part of the project staff, and any information shared with me would be kept confidential.

While it is unlikely that all the children present at the meeting understood clearly what I intended to do, at my next visit several youths volunteered to talk to me. In terms of order, as I came to realise afterwards, the first person I met was the 'President' of the youths, and those following close members of his 'bureau'. In order to help basic project management, the creation of a certain hierarchy amongst the children had been encouraged by the NGO, to facilitate collective interactions with the project staff. A 'President', a 'Treasurer', a 'Secretary', a 'Chief of Hygiene' had therefore been named by their peers and were mediating collective demands. During my subsequent visits, more and more children registered their names to schedule an interview with me,[15] probably reassured by what the early interviewees had reported to them and by my frequent visits to the centre. If one message had clearly been passed on, it was that I was not a threat.

2.2 Prevention, Demobilisation and Reintegration Programming

All of these children were involved in PDR activities at the time of the interviews. The project developed by the local NGO ODAFEM, under UNICEF auspices, was aimed at providing reinsertion support to children formerly associated with the FAFN. It targeted both official and self-demobilised children. The transition centre was located in Zélé, close to a FAFN major checkpoint, 5 km west of Man, in the renovated buildings of a former Christian mission.

The first step of the project entailed a three-month process, which included listening, counselling, individual profiling, medical care, sports, an initial career orientation session, basic numeracy and literacy[16] courses (refresher sessions for the already literate). During that period, demobilised children had to stay day and night in the transition centre, where they were offered proper care, shared accommodation, showering facilities, a functioning canteen, and basic entertainment (games, video). There were strict rules inside the centre premises; for instance, children had to ask for permission if they wanted to leave the centre to go somewhere else, even during the daytime.

The second step of the project consisted of a short-term vocational education programme. Youths were placed on a provisional basis at local entrepreneurs' workshops for a six-month period, at the end of which it was assumed that they had acquired the basics to continue the work they had learned themselves, with a starter kit of basic tools/inputs. During that phase, children had to leave the centre. Some were reunited with their families, while others were placed in foster care for the duration of the apprenticeship. The NGO had contacted local tailors, welders, hairdressers, auto and motor mechanics, and usually paid a monthly fee to the workshops' owners for accepting the apprenticed children. The canteen was no longer functional during that period, but children continued to receive assistance in the form of dry food through WFP donations. Rations were distributed monthly to each child and were calculated to be able to cover the nutritional needs of a family of six. When budget restrictions led the World Food Program to decrease its donations, they switched without notice from family to individual rations. This led to serious problems between some of the children and their fostering parents.

While reinsertion activities started in Man in February 2005, the reinsertion centre managed by ODAFEM was only operational in the summer of 2006. Not all children arrived in the centre at the same time (the self-demobilised in particular), but to facilitate basic logistics, they were regrouped in different 'waves'. At the time of the interviews, the first wave of children had already completed the three-month period at the centre and been placed in local entrepreneurs' workshops. I got access to some of their profiles. The children I interviewed were part of the second wave and had entered the project in the fall of 2006.

3   Pre-War Trajectories

The following three sections explore the pre-war, war and post-war trajectories of the youngest recruits and examine the profiles and motives that led children and adolescents to enlist with an armed group. Are there certain personal profiles more likely to engage in violent action? Do these profiles differ from those of adult combatants? What were the main incentives to join armed groups? Have younger recruits followed different patterns of mobilisation than their older peers, and do they exhibit different post-war trajectories?

In this part, I look at children's educational and professional trajectories before the war. I also explore the nature of their social networks and their relationships with their families before they joined pro-FAFN militias. Is there a causal relationship between pre-war profiles and processes of mobilisation? I prefer to argue that the two influence each other, to different extents, depending on individuals. A striking outcome of the interviews was the degree of resilience these children displayed when confronted with difficult situations. In sharp contrast with popular views, they were far from having few or no ties to society. They usually had a certain level of education and/or some job skills, as well as social connections, and were not necessarily more prone to violence than others.

3.1   Educational Trajectories

Some of the children I interviewed never went to school. A majority of the others had already quit school by the time the conflict started.[17] Reasons varied according to personal situations and included loss of interest in education, willingness to work, lack of means – especially after a parent's death, a family split, and at the end of the primary school phase, when the prospect of entering secondary school implied an impossible financial investment.

'My grandmother raised me. She put me into school. When she died, I moved to the village where my auntie lived. We were fourteen in the house. I stopped going to school, and I started helping her in the fields.'

'I was in CM2 before the war.[18] I took the secondary entrance exam, but I failed. My father was not rich. My older brother was in 5ème[19] and my sister in CM1, a year before me. In my village, it costs about 10,500 francs CFA to register for one year of schooling. So after I failed, I dropped out of school to help my father in his coffee plantation. The others continued.'

These accounts are not surprising per se. Education is not to be taken for granted in Côte d'Ivoire,[20] and for the ones who go to school, each additional year is the result of a fierce struggle against poverty and family priorities.[21] The majority of children were financially supported by their biological parents or by extended family in their education, but others were already fending for themselves. One respondent, for instance, was completely self-reliant at thirteen and was paying his school expenses himself. Another was supported by his grandfather in exchange for light agricultural work:

'When my grandmother died, I did not know who would take care of me. My father used to work in Abidjan, and he regularly sent money to her, but when he died – I was little – my grandmother was alone in taking care of me and of my older brothers. And then she died. I started fending for myself. I was doing some petty work to earn some cash to pay for my school.'

'I was in CE1 before the war. I used to live at my grandfather's place with my mother, my grandmother, my four older brothers and my sister. I was not staying with my father because he and my mother had split up. My grandfather used to pay for my school stationery and my schoolbooks. I had the reading book, the maths book, the history book and a homework notebook. At the end of every year, my grandfather was always giving me 5000 francs CFA to pay for new clothes. I used to work in his cocoa fields after school and during weekends and vacations. When it was harvest time, I picked the cocoa, let it dry, and then gave it to my grandfather to sell it to the purchasing clerks. That is how we paid for school.'

Children enrolled at school often held jobs from an early age, working usually during weekends and vacations but also sometimes after and before each school day. In rural areas, activities usually involved clearing fields, helping out during harvest time, and for the youngest, scaring away birds from the plantations. It was usually not seen as work, but as part of routine domestic chores.

> 'When the rice was maturing, I was going to the field every morning at 6 to scare the birds away from the plants. At 6:30, I returned to the village. School started at 8.'

> 'After school, I was not working. I was just helping my father in the fields. He had a coffee plantation. I also helped him grow rice, cassava, and yam.'

In urban areas, work was usually linked to an artisan workshop, with the aim of learning a skill and potential entry into the local labour market.

3.2 Professional Trajectories

Many respondents were engaged in a work activity at the time of their recruitment. They were not deriving an income from it, but it usually provided them with petty cash, even if it was not every day. The majority was working in agriculture, usually on family plantations (coffee, cocoa, maize or rice), and some had started to hire out their services to non-related people. Selling fruits, bush products or small items was also common to generate some income. Many respondents mentioned they already contributed to family expenses.

> 'I never went to school, we were too poor. I used to help my grandfather with his rice paddies. I started very young. He did not pay me, but at the end of every year, he always paid for my clothes.'

> 'When there was no school on Wednesday or Saturday, we used to go to the fields to pick bananas. We were selling them in the village. You can get 500 francs CFA for a full bag. With the money, we were paying for the school canteen, one dish at 25 francs CFA. The days we had money we stayed at school for lunch, we did not go back home. We played and then we went back to class in the afternoon.'

'I used to work in the family rice fields. I was also sometimes working on other people's plots. I could earn up to 2000 francs CFA a day. With that, I was paying for my clothes, my shoes, and I was giving the rest to my mother and my grandmother.'

'I had a bicycle. I used to sell ice-cold water on the road. I would fetch it first from some people I knew, then I would sell it retail. I could get 10,000 per day. 5000 I kept, 5000 I gave to the people who had given me the water.'

In urban and semi-urban areas, some children were engaged in apprenticeships, in local joiners', tailors', and mechanics' workshops. Hairdressing was popular, and not only with girls. Training was provided on the basis of family ties or against the payment of a tuition fee to acquaintances. Arrangements varied widely. Children were usually in their early teens when they started working for local entrepreneurs, and it was not rare for their place of work to be several kilometres away from their homes (especially when they came from a small village). This meant regularly commuting between home and work, and usually staying overnight at their boss's house or at some relative's place in town. Some of these youths had already dropped out of school. Others were still at school and were combining classes with job training.

'I know how to make wooden tables, chairs, stools, even beds. I have an uncle in town, 3 km away from my village, and I used to work in his workshop on weekends and vacations. He did not pay me when I was doing stuff for him. When I was doing work for me, I could sell a table for 1,500 francs CFA and a small case to keep coins for 100 francs. With that, I could buy my clothes. I did not have to pay for food as I was staying at my uncle's place. His wife prepared it. At the end of the vacations, he always gave me cash to pay for school.'

'My grandmother raised me. I never knew my father, and my mother died when I was 3 months old. We were poor. I dropped out of school when I was in CM2. I did not have the means to continue. Before her death, my grandmother put me in a job. I was eleven when I started welding. I used to go to work every morning. I learned by watching other people work. Sometimes, my boss would give me some tasks. I knew for instance how to make tables and iron doors. I was not paid. Sometimes, he gave me food; sometimes he didn't.'

Like many other countries, informal apprenticeships constitute the most common form of skills acquisition in Côte d'Ivoire. An estimated 450,000 young people are involved in such arrangements (Atchoarena and Delluc, 2002). Curiously though, these informal forms of job training tend not to be understood very well (Oketch, 2007). One standard pattern that came out of the discussions was that the boss (usually the one(s) owning the machines in the workshop) is the direct interface with clients. He has a list of orders to complete, and uses apprentices accordingly. The most skilled are usually able to complete most of the work and can be sent out from the workshop to handle major assignments. The less skilled watch the others working and can practise their techniques on simple repairs. In any workshop, there is a combination of low-skilled and high-skilled apprentices. Apprentices rarely receive cash for the work they do for the boss, apart from what they call '*prix du savon*', a small allowance usually not exceeding 100 to 200 francs CFA a day. This practice varies widely in individual cases and largely depends on the boss's degree of generosity. Apprentices who have already mastered some skills can usually use the machines in the workshop and after awhile work on their own orders, earning some cash by selling the products they make. Although this is not openly approved by the boss, the practice is nonetheless tolerated when all the boss's orders have been finished and when the boss is away from the workshop. A recurring habit is also to keep some of the payment when the boss is not around:

> 'My boss did not give me anything. It is when we were working 'behind him' that we could earn a bit for ourselves. You see, when we work, the boss wants to have all the money we earn. When it's like that, we are obliged to take out some money, otherwise we don't get anything. So for instance, a table like that costs 3000 francs CFA. I was taking a little part. When I was earning 2000 francs CFA, I usually kept 500 to myself and I gave 1,500 francs CFA to the boss.'

Several children also reported doing jobs in cities and towns, such as working as a salesman, pushing wheelbarrows (to carry luggage for someone else), or being involved in road maintenance:

> 'When it's rainy season, there are small rivers in the streets that carry a lot of sand. So I take a shovel and I dig the sand out. I sell it to construction workers.'

'I was pushing wheelbarrows. I could earn 1000 francs per day. It paid for my food and clothes.'

They usually kept a share for themselves and gave the rest to the parent they were closest to. Only a few children reported 'being too young' to do anything at all.

3.3   Relationships with the Family / Social Connectedness

Many respondents never lived with their nuclear family. They also often reported being dragged from one place to another because of changes in situation out of their control (such as their biological parents splitting up or dying). Some were living with their grandparents in situations of extreme poverty; others were staying with extended family, others with their biological parents. Many were using loose networks to get along from day to day and could not rely on close family support. At this point, I do not want to suggest that these children were disconnected socially or that this was a specific feature of children who enrolled in the military (it unfortunately is the fate of many poor people). What I would rather stress is the surprising resilience and maturity these children displayed when confronted with difficult situations. A few accounts were quite extreme, with children being left on their own at very young ages, due to complex situations and tension in the family.

> 'I first stayed with my mother, in the village. Then she sent me to school in town, and I stayed at my aunt's. She was single – like my mother – and had two other children. My mother was paying for my school stationery and sometimes sent rice to my aunt's from the village. My aunt was preparing food for me. One day, my auntie told me to go back to my village. She had too many expenses. When I went back, my mother told me to go back to town and to learn a skill. She sent me to someone she knew. He had a tailoring workshop, and I stayed at his place. It lasted one year. Then my boss moved to another town with his family, and I lost contact with him. When he left, I started doing small jobs in town. I was pushing wheelbarrows. I could earn 1000 francs per day. It paid for my food and clothes. I had another relative in town, the son of my uncle, and I was staying at his place.'

> 'When my mother died – I was six or seven – they sent me to an uncle, near Abidjan, but then he died, and I had to come back to my father, in the village. I was in my second year of primary school. I don't know why

but the other people in the village disliked my father. There were always disputes, even with his family. And then he abandoned me. He had an argument with his wife, and he told me to move out of the house. I was no longer his son. I started hanging around in the village, sleeping outside, doing some work in the fields for people to get food. After a while I decided to move to the village of my mother's parents. I did not last too long. I eventually decided to take my chance in town. In Man, I met some people. They are not family, but they helped me. I pray with them.'

4 Wartime Experiences

In this part, I look at the complexity of the processes leading to children's mobilisation and at the different motives that drove them into armed groups. I also describe some of their experiences with warfare.

4.1 Motivations to Join

The youngest recruits mentioned various reasons for joining in the rebellion, ranging from self-defence to the protection of parents, passing through revenge, lack of alternatives, and merely seizing an opportunity to secure food for a limited period of time. Some enlisted late and only joined the military after a brother or sister had done so, several months prior. Some were recruited because they were alone, with no resources, in a place full of soldiers. For them, joining the army was a logical move, and in such circumstances, becoming a soldier is likely to be perceived as a necessary and positive choice for children. 'When there is a total breakdown of society, armed groups may provide the only source of refuge and safety' (Rosen, 2007).

Motives were rarely clear-cut, and respondents usually brought forward more than one reason in their narrative, pointing to different degrees of agency. As an analyst, I started wondering if some motives weighed more heavily than others in their decision-making and if I should rank them in my interpretation. I quickly discarded that option. What led children into the group and kept them there was the result of a complex process rather than attributable to isolated factors. What mattered in the end was how respondents made sense of their war experience, and how they interpreted their entry into the groups and their stay there. With some children, it was clear from their accounts that they never wanted to be where they were. The ones who were coerced by Liberian mercenaries, for instance, were forced to do things that they would have despised in normal times (torturing prisoners, extortion, stealing). These youths reported feeling under constant threat. With other children, it was more complex. Even if some had been abducted for the movement, they did not experience their belonging to the group as something entirely negative.

The accounts that follow describe the complex reasons and processes that led very young people to engage in violence. They clearly show that the phenomenon of child soldiering cannot be reduced to coerced recruits, and that even the youngest can exercise some degree of reflection and agency when enlisting in the military.[22] Two primary aims of respondents were staying alive and protecting their closest caregiver, which in practice meant finding the right strategies when their path and the military's crossed. The testimonies are expressive enough to give a fair idea of the diversity of enlistment patterns while bringing to the fore the extraordinary individual stories. Some of the accounts have been slightly adapted for better reader comprehension.

The most logical response to a direct threat

'The war came in the weekend. I was in town, working in my uncle's workshop. Everybody fled. I fled with my cousin. We went to the bush, then to the village. My uncle was there. He told us that he feared he would get robbed. He did not have the time to lock his home. The attack arrived so quick that even the food had stayed on the stove. So with my cousin, we went back to town to guard the houses. We stayed in one home, and we were watching the others. One day, a rebel came. He told us not to worry and that he would stay with us. We would eat together. After a while another rebel came, and then another. Eventually, there were a lot of them in the house. My cousin said we'd better join them. We were stuck anyway. We could not go back to the village because they had installed checkpoints.'

'Everybody had fled the village, but I had stayed with my grandfather. When the rebels came, they said my grandfather was hiding a soldier at his place. They started to beat him up. I pitied him. I even cried. They shot a bullet at his feet. But they had lied. He was hiding no-one. They searched everywhere in the house. They told my grandfather that they would kill him if he had not told them the truth. That is why I joined the rebellion. It hurt me to watch my grandfather being molested. Two or three days after this incident, me and my brother gave our names, and we joined the rebels.'

'When the rebels came into town, there were gunshots everywhere. I took my sister to our village. Shortly after, the rebels arrived there. They asked the youngest: "Who is the village chief? Who has money here?" They were threatening us. I wanted to defend my parents so I told my brother I wanted to join the rebels. He said no and advised me not to, but I said, maybe I will succeed in the rebellion. God will decide.'

'The rebels stayed four months in my village. They were all Liberians. I used to hang out around them. They used to send me to buy food, cigarettes… They used to beat parents. I joined so they would leave my father alone. One day, they wanted to take my father's chickens to eat. I said: "No, these are from my father, leave them." And they told my father "Fine, your son is with us, we are not going to take your hens. Give us one and we eat together." My father gave them a chicken. It was a gift, it was not taken by force.'

Coercion

'When the rebels came, they took people by force and loaded them into trucks. They caught me and my brother. We did not want to go, but we had to. They were threatening people at gunpoint.'

'I was at school when the rebels entered my village. It was three in the afternoon. I was alone in the classroom. It was recreation time so my friends were outside. I was inside because I was doing my homework in advance. My friends had time to flee to the bush, but the rebels caught me and the teacher. Eventually, they only took me. I spent three years with them. I was the only one to be taken from my village.'

'They caught me one morning. I was going to the field to take some cassava, and they saw me pass. They told me: "Where are you going?" I told them I was going to the field. They told me to go with them in their truck. I was scared. They had guns. I was obliged to go. They brought us to Danané.'

Lack of alternatives

'I was recruited by someone I knew from my neighbourhood. He knew my difficulties. My grandmother had died, and she was the one who used to take care of me. My boss had also died, and I had to stop my work at the workshop. When the rebels took the town, my neighbour joined them, right from the beginning. When he saw that he was earning a bit of money, he came back to our neighbourhood to recruit people. He knew my situation. He told me to go with him; he told me I would earn something out of it. He promised me money.'

'I was sharing a room in town with the son of my uncle. He used to sell stuff at the market, and I was earning petty cash by pushing wheelbarrows. He was paying for the rent. He did not ask me anything, and I did not ask him anything. We were fending for ourselves. When the rebels came, they took my cousin, and when I next saw him, he was in "treillis" [in combat uniform]. The town was empty, most people had fled. So when my cousin saw me, he took me with him. He told me that, because of the war, it would be better for me to stay in the military camp, not in the house, because if I stayed alone in the house, something bad could happen to me. After a while in the camp, I became a rebel.'

'My sister had joined the rebels and had moved to another village with them. These days, there was not much to eat in the village, and we did not know how to cope. My sister used to send us one bag of rice at the end of every month. With that, we could eat. One day, she came back for a visit with her boyfriend. He was also a rebel. She told me to go with her. She was preparing food in the camp. I was helping her boyfriend at checkpoints.'

4.2 Actions in Warfare

Only a few respondents participated in combat activities, but those who did were the first on the front lines, and listening to their experiences made me realise what the expression 'cannon fodder' literally meant. Other actions linked to warfare included carrying guns and ammunition, working in shifts guarding military bases day and night, torturing prisoners, shaking down civilians at checkpoints, looting goods, and acting as bodyguards for adult commanders, which I later interpreted as quite an honorary position for being sometimes used as a human shield. Children also reported performing various logistical tasks during their stay in the military, such as cooking, washing, fetching food, cigarettes, or drugs for older recruits, and escorting women to local markets to pick up basic supplies for the camp.

Children's accounts reveal that they were the ideal scapegoats for anything that went wrong. If some older recruit had lost something or reported a theft, they were accused. If they disagreed with their chief (which usually meant the man who recruited them, not necessarily the chief of their section), they were beaten up. During interviews, they were in fact particularly open in showing their scars and telling how they had come by them. To avoid harm, most of them adopted an acceptance strategy during their time in the group, which mainly consisted of obeying orders, minimising unnecessary interactions with older recruits, and enduring punishment passively when it came. Violence was an integral feature of their daily routine and ranged from verbal abuse to the cruellest of acts. Respondents recruited by Liberian mercenaries witnessed and performed the most barbaric acts.

Some respondents had tried to allay some of their stress and regain partial control of their lives. Some would look for places where they could be alone, others disobeyed orders, for instance the order not to loot. These were precious moments that acted as a safety valve, relieving some of the pressure, regardless of the consequences (which were often painful for the child when caught).

The testimonies presented below show the diversity of the activities respondents were engaged in during their stay in the military and the resilience they displayed in coping with extremely stressful situations. The recurrent use of 'us' and 'they' in children's narratives is rather striking and is an illustration of their awareness of being treated specially in the group.

Actions

> 'I was cooking for them. They were sending me sheep and chickens to prepare and then we ate together.'

> 'I used to pull the harrow at checkpoints.'

> - I wounded people, I killed. My chief told me that whenever I hear shootings or when it becomes violent, I must shoot, not to be killed myself. He taught me how to shoot. I obeyed.
> - Interviewer: What else were you doing? Were you also at checkpoints? Were you doing guard shifts at the camp?
> - Respondent: No. What you are talking about, that happened later, when the situation calmed down. We were there when there was fighting in

town. There was no camp yet, no checkpoint. We were in the front line, to push back the enemy. We did not want to murder people. We just wanted to push them back and take the town. But when attacked, we were obliged to defend ourselves. I saw a lot of my friends die.'

'We were guarding their guns. If they had to go somewhere, they would leave us behind at the checkpoint, to watch their weapons. They would warn us not to give anything to other rebels who might come to us.'

'I was keeping records of the cargo that came in and out the camp. It was military cargo; soldiers would jump in and would leave for combat. For instance, if I count 15, I write 15 in the book and then I tell the chief. I also told recruits when they had to go to take their shift at checkpoints. There was a special book for that. For instance, if some had to work on Monday, I would go and tell them. People would listen, no problem.'

'Some days, they were saying: "Come on children, you are going to help us carrying some luggage and loading trucks." We say: "OK." We go with them by car, we load trucks, and we would come back to the base. Then they go into town to sell.'

'We used to molest thieves and prisoners. We would injure them with knives. When I had to hurt someone and if I felt sorry for him, I smoke drugs beforehand, to force myself.'

'My chief told me to break into the houses people had left to steal things. Our commander did not like that, but I was obliged to do it because it was an order from my chief. We used to search everywhere in the houses. I had to give everything to my chief. I was not allowed to sell the stuff myself. If the chief was in a good mood, he would give me some money. If not, I got nothing. Sometimes, I kept small things for me. I kept a Walkman and a tape player.'

'I was doing patrols. Sometimes, we were told that some recruits were bothering people in a village nearby, that they were stealing from them. We would go there, on patrol. We would take the recruits back to the base, by force if necessary. On our way back, we often got permission to beat them, in the truck.'

'We used to search people, inspect luggage and trucks. If we see someone with a weapon, we hurt him. If we see someone with no identity card, we hold him and put him to work. He can sweep the floor for instance and we take his money.'

'We were the ones who knew the area best. We knew where people would hide their cars. We would show them.'

Punishments

'They were beating us a lot, especially when the chief was not here. Every single thing that went wrong with him, it was for us. They were saying: "Your chief did this and this…, where is he…?", and then they were beating us.'

'The way they used to tie people up was really scary. They tied the hands behind the back, exposing the breast, the life, like a chicken. They used to tie us up. One day, the chief left his Walkman next to where we were, at the checkpoint. When he came back, he looked for it. He was told that one of us had taken it. They started beating us, the Walkman did not reappear. The one who had taken it had already gone away. So they tied us up saying that we were telling lies.'

'They beat me only once, in the beginning, but very strong. They wanted me to smoke some special cigarette and I did not want it, so they beat me. You can see my injuries. They hit me with a cane and also hurt me with iron. They heated it on a fire, and then they put it on me. I also have knife cuts.'

Resilience

'At checkpoints, our chiefs told us to give them all the money we took from people because they had to buy food for us for the evening. But if I got much, I split the money and hid some for myself.'

'We could never sleep in the rebellion. I had to flee to take a nap in the fields. There, I could sleep a little. I always came back afterwards. Sometimes, they caught me out in the fields. They beat me up. They used their fists, or ropes, or belts.'

5 Post-War Trajectories

Research on children's and adolescents' processes of demobilisation has largely remained confined to the examination of external interventions – with the main pitfall being to overestimate the impact of projects in the children's reinsertion phase and to largely ignore the role of endogenous features. In this part, I look at children's processes of demobilisation within and outside program frameworks. What drove them to leave the armed groups? Do they exhibit different post-war trajectories than their older peers? How did they make use of the reinsertion prospects that external interventions offered? How did – or did they not – integrate them with other opportunities faced at the same time?

5.1 Demobilisation

Demobilisation accounts varied a lot depending on the individuals, ranging from mere escape, to open self-demobilisation, as well as cases of commanders directly handing over recruits to humanitarian staff. Some respondents stayed a few months with rebel forces, while others stayed for several years. In many accounts, children's length of stay in the armed group was linked to the length of stay of the group in the area. When there was a move to establish the base in another location, rebels often took some children with them while letting others go.

Triggers to demobilisation usually included discussions with caregivers, the visit of a parent to the camp, a change in command, the death of the direct chief, seizing an opportunity to escape (absence of chief, not returning from leave), and the emergence of children's critical consciousness in extremely violent contexts ('it is not worth staying, I can be killed tomorrow'). In some cases, release was negotiated by a family member. When bargaining was not possible or when the child had no one to bargain for him, a risky escape and the ability to profit from external interventions were the only way out. In the group of respondents recruited by Liberian mercenaries, several respondents reported having taken advantage of the period when Liberians were driven out of Côte d'Ivoire by the Ivoirian rebels to return to civilian life.

Escape

'I did not feel safe. They were killing people in front of me. When I was sleeping, I was dreaming a lot. My head was not good. I fell sick. I told my chief I wanted to look after myself so I went to my grandmother's. But he came and brought me back to his house. I used to work for him, sweep his floor, prepare his food... I left a second time and that time, my grandmother hid me. When they came to look for me, she told them she did not know where I was. But they told her that she should not lie otherwise they would kill her. She showed them where I was, in a village nearby. I was sick anyway. I could not even get up. When my chief saw me, he told me to come back to him when I was better. I waited two months before returning to my village. When I heard that my chief had eventually left our village, I went back to my grandmother's. She cured me.'

'My sister's boyfriend was a rebel. When he left the camp on a mission, we fled. We did not ask for permission. We took things. My sister took a radio to bring to the village. She had some money so she paid for our transport. We avoided the checkpoint. We took a car that was heading to Man. When we arrived in Man, we continued directly to our village.'

'At first, I did not want to quit. My friends were there, we were together, we were happy. But when they started to beat us up when they thought we had stolen things, I got scared. I realised that they could tell lies about me and that they could kill me. It happened to someone I knew from my village. They killed him because he was accused of having stolen a radio. But it was not him. And the Liberians, they showed no pity. That is why I quit.'

Self-demobilisation

'When my chief was killed, I was in my village with permission, I was visiting my family. I decided to stay there. They did not come to look for me.'

'I requested permission to visit my parents in the village. I did not want to go back to the rebel forces, but they came to look for me. I told them I could not go with them, but they caught me and sent me to town. The second time I got permission, I told them I had no time to go with them because I had started agricultural work with my father. They let me go.'

'My mother visited me in the camp. She asked me to quit. She told me she would find me work. I listened to her, and I left the camp. I had no problem to leave. I talked to my commander, and I told him I was tired of the life in the camp. I told him I wanted to go home. He was fine with that. He brought me to the Etat Major to tell his chief, and they let me go.'

'My chief had a lot of debts and had failed to pay back those higher in command. He was killed because of that. I saw it. I quit right after. My chief had told me that he would give me money, but now that he had died, I told myself that I would not get anything and that I might die as well if I stayed in the rebellion. It was not a problem to leave. They did not hold me back. They did not give me money either. To get some cash, I sold the small handgun I had to a rebel. For 50,000.'

'In the rebellion, I was with the Liberians. When they were driven out, I left them, and I came to Man. I arrived at night. I went to the camp. I was asked if I was a soldier. I said that I was a soldier before, with the Liberians, but that I had left them. Then an old rebel said that because I was a rebel before, I could stay and sleep in the camp, we were all soldiers. He also said that after the war, there would be projects, small things; he would help me get into those. Then he said that his wife was also Yacouba, like me, and that I should visit her. When I told her my mother's name, she told me that she knew my mother. She took me in her house, and I stopped sleeping in the camp. I still eat there sometimes.'

Externally driven demobilisation

'When I heard that UNICEF was going to take care of the children who were with the rebels, I came to town to give my name. At that time, I used to be stationed between the airport and the checkpoint, near Zélé.'

'I wanted to quit the rebel forces, but I could not. Because once, one man told them he wanted to quit, and they killed him in front of me. I was scared. There were other children in the camp, but for them, there was no problem in leaving because they often had brothers in the rebel forces who could negotiate their departure with the chief. I had no brother in the rebel forces, so I was obliged to stay. They never gave me permission when I asked for it to visit my parents. If UNICEF had not come with the project, I would still be in the camp.'

5.2 Social Reinsertion

How smooth was their return to civil life? Accounts were mixed in terms of community acceptance, and while some respondents reported having experienced extreme rejection by their direct environment, others mentioned having been warmly welcomed from the start. Although a whole range of reactions was reported, the stigma attached with belonging to an armed group may have been greater for girls; however, we lack extensive girls' testimonies. Some were clearly isolated upon return, feared or mocked; others could easily blend in. In line with other studies (Save the Children, 2004), the role of parents, caregivers and, in some cases, village chiefs has often been the major factor in putting an end to verbal abuse and isolation, and in mediating the social reinsertion of the youth. A few respondents mentioned having gone through some kind of cleansing ritual shortly after their return home, to purify them of their wrong-doing, and of taking part in warfare.

Another important feature is that many children never totally cut their military ties after their demobilisation, with some continuing to interact with soldiers on a daily basis, especially in towns where military camps were based. Several respondents were in fact hosted by older recruits. In some cases, their mother – or foster parent – was living with a soldier husband or boyfriend. In others, their mothers were cooking in one of the military camps, and they were often going there, if only for food.

These examples challenge current ideas about demobilisation. A common pitfall is in fact to take military and post-military lives as two completely different matters, two different spaces, with few links between them. In many contexts though, it is difficult to draw such a line and to stop all kinds of interaction between armed groups and non-armed ones. In Man for instance, an urban setting which is home to several military camps, soldiers have become part of the town and are part of the direct environment of its residents. Some are full-time recruits, while others work outside the military. They earn a living, and they could even be seen as civilians when they are not on duty.

Relationships neighbourhood / family

'When my sister and I returned to our village, my mother told me that I was no longer her child. She had told me not to join the rebels, and I had not listened to her. Why? She was not happy. But then my grandfather forgave me, and she accepted. My grandfather called my mother and told her: 'What the child did, it is not his fault. It is his sister's fault because she asked him to follow her.' They did not forgive my sister. She left the day after our return. She slept, then she left, without telling anyone.'

'When we went back to our parents, they were very happy. Nobody bothered us. They thought that we were dead, that we had already been killed. I moved back in with my father and mother. I started helping my mother in the fields. My father was sick and had stopped working.'

'They were all scared of me. They would not come close to me because they thought I was violent, I could kill someone. They were scared. I was mostly alone. I was sad. I had no friends. When she saw that, my tutrice [caregiver] gathered the people in the neighbourhood to ask them forgiveness. She told them that I would not harm them and that they could play with me. Now it is OK. I have no problem anymore.'

'In my village, everyone knows I was a rebel. Here in town, some people know, some people don't. It was not a problem because I was never stationed in Man when I was in the rebel forces. I was close to the Liberian border. Here I have no contacts anymore with soldiers. I play football, everyday at 5 p.m., after I'm done with work.'

'It did not go well in the beginning with people in my village. I did not feel well. I could not approach them. My head was not good. I was not talking to anyone. I wanted to become old. I was not good.'

'People were bothering us in the village. They were saying that we were rebels, that we were the rebels' wives. Even my friends used to say that. So

I told my parents. They told the village chief. The Chief told the people not to say that anymore. They told my friends not to mock me. It is now good.'

Cleansing rituals

'After I left the rebels, I spent two months alone. I was staying in town. The third month, my tutrice found me. She had searched for me in the beginning, but with the war in town, she could not find me, and because of the fear of being shot by a stray bullet, she mostly stayed at home. When it was calmer, she resumed her search, and she found me. The same day, I moved back with her. She gave me advice. She insulted me. She told me to take off everything I wore. I stripped, I changed clothes, I washed myself well. She gave me food. I ate.'

Continued interaction with armed groups

'I live with my mother. She is preparing food at the camp. She has a boyfriend. He is also a low-ranked recruit. It goes well. She usually comes back home in the evening. She is not preparing lunch for us. When I have some cash, I eat in town. But sometimes, when I see that I don't have enough, I go and eat in the camp.'

'I used to live with the mother of a friend of mine. One day, a rebel came. He was looking for a room to rent. The mother of my friend said that she had a spare room he could use, behind the house. He agreed and set his mattress inside. But then, a radio disappeared. We were accused, but we thought that the rebel had stolen it. We went to see him, with a friend of ours who is also in the military. He is the boyfriend of my friend's sister. He beat him up. We also beat him up. He finally told us that he had already given the radio away.'

'I stay with an adjutant here. He is the brother of my mother. He is a soldier. It goes well. He said that if I get a sewing machine with the project, he will help me to set up my workshop.'

5.3 Going Back to School?

It might challenge a few existing ideas, but relatively few respondents indicated that they wanted to go back to school. Of the 23 cases that were still in school when the war started, and only a minority resumed their education inside or outside a project framework. Reasons brought forward usually included age, 'being too old' and not having the mindset for studying after their stay with the rebel forces. The bulk of the respondents preferred learning a skill or improving a skill they already had. Most had already lost several years to the rebellion, which had brought them little benefit; they therefore strongly expressed their willingness to stop wasting their time.

> 'I don't want to go back to school. I can't go back to school. I want a job, I need to earn a living. I'd rather learn a skill than go back to primary school. I feel too sorry for myself for what happened.'

> 'I'm too old now to go to CE1.'

> 'When I came back to the village, I went back to school to try the CEPE [secondary-entrance exam]. I did a whole year at school, but I failed the exam. And then I dropped out. If I get support, I would like to continue, but now, I don't have books.'

This puts the myth of school as salvation into perspective and questions the stance that education is the ideal cure for preventing children from returning to armed groups as is suggested by many statements taken from institutional reports: 'Without adequate educational opportunities, these children will remain vulnerable to the parasite economic interests of their commanders' (Human Rights Watch, 2005). 'Having access to school reduces the boredom and idleness that encourages children to seek a more exciting life' (Save the Children, 2005). So few children opt for resuming their education – with good reason – that one has to question why schooling is overemphasised as an external intervention, at the expense of other options that appear more relevant to the young involved. Equating 'not going to school' with 'boredom' and 'idleness' is a rather simplistic view which distorts the youth's pre-war trajectories and oversimplifies the processes leading to their mobilisation. As mentioned earlier, most respondents were not idle at the time of their recruitment and were already engaged in some kind of work.[23]

5.4 Reinserting Through and Outside Projects

In practice, one standard response is to offer catch-up classes for those who are still of school age (a large minority), to allow them to reintegrate into the formal school system. For those too old to return to school, short-term vocational training remains the norm. Both options rarely deliver long-term results. Only a minority finds the financial means to continue schooling to post-primary levels, and learning a skill requires several years, unless the skill was already known before the war. Also, it might raise expectations that cannot always be met (substantial investment is needed in some cases, especially when learning joining and welding, and external interventions are usually reluctant to make substantial expenses).[24] Short-term training and basic kits are usually not sufficient to secure a sustainable livelihood. If the youths who receive that help cannot find the financial means necessary to buy the additional equipment to start their own workshop (usually the most expensive), they are condemned to remaining confined to extremely low-paid apprenticeships. In contrast, owning equipment opens many doors.

Arrangements in workshops varied a lot, depending on individuals. In some cases, the boss provided lunch and gave apprentices petty cash at the end of the day (100-200 francs CFA). Some always did that, while others only did so occasionally. In other cases, the boss gave nothing.

> 'On days there is a lot of work, we cannot go back home for lunch. So the boss gives us money. Days when there is not a lot of work, he gives nothing. It really depends. When he gives, he gives 150-250 francs CFA.'

Respondents who already had some skills could usually earn a bit. Apprentice tailors would repair clothes at home, apprentice joiners would make basic furniture to sell, and apprentice hairdressers would braid acquaintances' hair at home.

One important issue that arises when apprentices are placed in workshops by NGOs (and not by relatives) is how to ensure the continuity of the training when NGO support ends. As said earlier, the local NGO which had been providing these children support had contacted local tailors, welders, hairdressers, auto and motor mechanics, and was paying a monthly fee to the workshops' owners to accept the apprentices. When apprentices were placed by relatives, arrangements usually varied a lot. They generally included the payment of tuition fees, but on a much more flexible basis. So when the project came to a halt in late 2007, arrangements had to be renegotiated by the apprentice or his/her relatives. When the boss was happy with the apprentice's work, it was not a problem, but when the boss was unhappy, or when there were too few customers for the workshop, several respondents had to stop.

> 'My boss, she wants to keep me. She told me that when the project finishes, we will talk. She'll tell me how much I have to pay to stay.'

> 'After the project, I would like to continue in the same tailoring workshop. I am good at it. I can cut fabrics, and sew trousers and blouses. Usually it takes two years to learn how to cut. The boss told me that I could stay. When I am good enough, my uncle told me that he would help me to set up my own workshop.'

Longitudinal follow-up of some of the children gave some interesting results. Out of the 21 boys and girls whom I interviewed in December 2006 and June 2007, 15 had ended their activity two years later and were doing something else, while six were continuing on the same track (even when they changed workshops in between). This is a pattern we also find with adult recruits who entered reinsertion projects (Chelpi-den Hamer, 2009a). Many stopped the activity or 'disappeared' out of sight of the project staff a few months after being placed in certain reinsertion tracks. Sometimes, there is nothing wrong. Understandably, when more interesting opportunities emerge elsewhere, or when familial obligations must be met, these will take up the project participants' time and attention. Other times, it is more complex. Not continuing an activity can be linked to stigma (being known as a former recruit), discrimination (being labelled idle or a thief), or lack of means (lacking the money to pay the tuition fee to the workshop owner). Such behaviour must therefore not be interpreted as deviant, and development actors have a genuine interest in understanding what motivates participants to divert from their initial reinsertion stream. It can pave the way to better programming.

> 'My first boss kicked me out. He said that I did not come regularly to work, that I did not come soon enough. It was true. Everyday, he wanted me to come at 8 a.m. and I arrived at 9 a.m. He was usually sending me away, saying, 'We do not work like that here.' The days I was not working, I have a friend here, a military, he has TV, DVD. He often calls us to watch movies. With my second boss, that was something else. A relative from my village had come to town and had seen that I was doing nothing. I explained that my boss had kicked me out. He told me that he had a friend

who had a garage nearby and that he could introduce me to him. I worked there for a month. After a while, my boss asked me about my former job. He asked me who had placed me there. I told him everything, that an NGO had put me there. He asked me to come back with my supervisor. I told him, but he did not show up. So I stopped working.'

'I never received my kit because I moved to another town. It was hard to stay in Man. We did not have a lot of means with my tutrice, and it was difficult to make ends meet. So I wanted to fend for myself. I followed an apprentice I knew, from the workshop, when he set up his own workshop in the nearby town. I'm staying at his brother's place. I still work in welding, and I am second in command in the workshop. I don't have many things to learn anymore, I know the skills. I used to work in welding before the war, and it's been more than two years since I resumed work. Now, I would like to set up my own workshop. I know people in Abidjan, former apprentices, who told me that I could go and work with them when I have my own equipment. They can find me a place to set me up.'

'At the end of the project, they gave us one kit for two, one sewing machine. It was not good. As the person with whom I was sharing the machine had to move elsewhere, we sold it for 50,000 francs CFA, and we split 25,000 – 25,000. That's how I gave up tailoring. Six months ago, I got an opportunity to work as an apprentice driver. I asked someone, and he agreed to take me. I am now travelling a lot, Man, Daloa, Korhogo, Odienné, and often for several days. We're always on the road unless there is a problem with the truck. My boss gives me between 4,000 and 6,000 per trip, depending. He feeds me too, while we are away. When I'm back in town, I no longer live with my mother. I rent a room for 2,500 a month, in the quartier Belleville. I have a girlfriend. She is pregnant.'

6 Concluding Remarks & Reflections on Child Soldiering

Younger recruits do not necessarily follow different patterns of mobilisation and demobilisation than their older peers, and any statement that claims so must be challenged by empirical evidence. Do their pre-war profiles differ? Perhaps the main difference with adult recruits is that child recruits experience a substantial loss in terms of human capital, which adults generally do not (Blatmann, 2006). In our case, the ones at school when the conflict started and the ones involved in apprenticeships clearly wasted precious years; as they say, 'They put themselves late.' Their involvement in warfare postponed their individual social advancement. While their pre-war trajectories shared some similarities with their older peers (Chelpi-den Hamer, 2009b), the main differences included the financial dependence of most respondents (even if many were contributing to the family income), and a limited geographical mobility. Adult respondents often reported having left home in their late teens or early twenties, in search of better prospects elsewhere. With child respondents, this was much less pronounced, due to their young age.

In terms of recruitment, children clearly expressed more fear, even when they could exercise some kind of agency in the process. Processes of mobilisation were complex, there was no single pattern, and they generally challenged popular theories on social movement that tend to assume a causal relationship between pre-war backgrounds and motives for enlistment. Do child recruits exhibit specific post-war trajectories? One difference with adults, partly due to their loss of human capital at an early age, is that children and adolescents usually had less time to acquire a skill before the war and had not yet had time to develop a large social network. This usually resulted in having fewer options after the war, for employment or self-employment. Although one would expect that this would be a motive to embrace the opportunities humanitarian interventions offer (by working hard during their training, by showing they are motivated, by being willing to continue learning skills, by being assiduous), longitudinal follow-up of some of the children provides a different picture and shows high dropout rates. Clearly, reinsertion assistance has to be redefined in order to bear any fruit.

External interventions had a very mixed impact on the lives of the former recruits we interviewed. One important effect was that they boosted the number of demobilisations. Some children self-demobilised when they heard that they had the option to register for a project; others were directly referred to humanitarian staff by military commanders; and others were traced back to their village when NGOs toured war-affected areas to provide some kind of support to children formerly associated with armed forces.[25] Another positive impact is that it provided short-term relief to children entering a reinsertion project, by supplying them with food on a daily basis, medical care, and school supplies for the minority who resumed schooling plus some kind of job counselling.

In other aspects, the impact was rather mitigated. Interventions only played a marginal role in facilitating children's social reinsertion, especially since several children had joined the project several years after their demobilisation, usually after a period at home when they experienced the most difficulties associated with the reintegration into their communities. A whole range of reactions was reported. For some, it went rather smoothly; they were warmly welcomed from the start, and they could easily blend in. Others reported experiencing extreme forms of rejection. They were clearly isolated upon return, feared and/or mocked. The actions of parents, caregivers and village chiefs have been, in these cases, most important in putting a halt to verbal abuse and isolation and in mediating their social reinsertion.

With children involved in job training, projects have tended to miss the dynamics of these young people's lives, by perceiving negatively those who dropped out of the activity or who moved on to other things, and by showing a limited interest in seeking to understand what motivated them to do so (Donais, 2007; Jennings, 2007; Lee, 2009; Long, 2001).

6.1 Reflections on Child Soldiering

Despite the fact that young people have been present on the battlefield for centuries, in both Western and non-Western contexts, child soldiering has recently been presented as a new and massive phenomenon, with rough estimates of 250,000 under-age recruits worldwide, located mainly in developing countries. It has come to be very negatively perceived internationally (Rosen, 2007). There are several debates associated with the youngest combatants, which are worth reflecting upon, keeping this case study in mind. One of these indeed relates to free choice and the extent to which children and adolescents exercise their own agency when they enlist in armed groups (Peters et al., 2003). Another controversy concerns the age marker of 18, and the extent to which it is relevant to make a distinction between child and adult combatants using such a tool, especially when processes of demobilisation occur within the framework of external interventions, which entitle children and adults to different benefits. I reflect on those points below.

Informed choice
There are a number of statements about children which nowadays cannot be refuted without being considered socially incorrect. Across contexts, they are usually presented as innocent, vulnerable, dependent, regardless of their lived realities, to the point that it has become unimaginable that they can make a rational choice which involves them in evil actions. Boyden has rightly pointed out that any child engaged in violence disturbs adults, foremost because by going against the odds, he/she challenges the very foundation of the existing social order (Boyden, 2007). In the same vein, Honwana recognises that children who behave violently clearly fall outside mainstream formulations of childhood and upset social norms and codes (Honwana, 2005). The view that children are innocent is largely based on a certain conception of children's cognitive development that assumes that their moral understanding, their political thoughts and their actions differ widely from those of adults because they mature in stages, following an ordered sequence of cognitive steps (Kohlbert, 1976; Piaget, 1972). In this perspective, children's abilities to think and act reasonably are largely immune from environmental influence, a lower age limit is suggested for linking moral reasoning with action, and adolescents and pre-pubescent youth are considered to be more malleable than adults. Child soldiering is mainly explained through coercion, abuse of authority, unscrupulous commanders or drug addiction. Some agencies have openly taken the stand that under-18s are in any case forced into armed groups, because before that age 'children cannot be considered to have the maturity to make an informed decision to join an armed force' (Human Rights Watch, 1996). Institutional reports and some scholarly works have also contributed to shaping public opinion on this theme by tending to be lacking in nuance in their analysis, and by emphasizing certain patterns to the detriment of others (Betancourt

et al., 2008; Brett and McCallin, 1996; Brett and Specht, 2004; Denov, 2005; Machel, 1996; Singer, 2006).

Far from denying that children's recruitment is the result of coercion in many cases, and that some children took part in atrocities when they were soldiers, reducing their agency to none during their enlistment process and during the war is not the only option. In line with recent research (Boyden, 2007; Rosen, 2005), this case study shows that children in different cultures are likely to engage in complex moral reasoning at a much younger age than expected. This is in sharp contrast with the former view, which suggested a lower age limit for linking thoughts to actions. In developing countries in particular, where most people are used to fending for themselves from an early age, context and experience play a major role in the development of human cognition and in influencing modes of action. In this perspective, there is no universal definition of childhood, and the concept is locally defined. Children are no longer presented as passive subjects but as active agents of their own development, able to form and express opinions and participate in decision-making processes in matters concerning themselves. Age and maturity do not necessarily go hand in hand, and adulthood is no longer idealised by overestimating grown-ups' immunity to being influenced. Child soldiering is not solely explained in terms of physical coercion and intimidation, and the complexity of reasons and processes that lead very young people to engage in violence has finally come to be acknowledged (Hart, 2009).

The 18 marker
Age limit has become an important benchmark with respect to using children as soldiers, and in the late 1990s, there was considerable debate on which minimum age for recruitment to set in international law.[26] A range of actors actively lobbied for abolishing the marker of the age of 15 as the minimum tolerated age for recruitment, and for raising this age limit to 18 in official documents (Harvey, 2000). Mainstream discourse dismissed children's political and social agency in their participation in warfare and centred on concepts that emphasised the innocence and victimhood of the child (Lee, 2009). INGOs were particularly active in pushing this view, along with the International Committee of the Red Cross, the Swedish government and the Quaker UN Office in Geneva (Brett, 2005; Rosen, 2007). In favour of the change, proponents argued that the 1989 UN Convention of the Rights of the Child had failed to completely prohibit child recruitment. It was also leading to confusion as it defined a child as anyone under 18, in need of special protection,

while at the same time it tolerated recruitment of 16- and 17-year-olds. This anomaly had to be corrected. Opponents feared that too much focus on age would distract international attention from more fundamental issues such as forced recruitment, notably arguing that what mattered was the way conscription took place, not chronological age (Ryle, 1999). Whether recruits were 16, 18 or 21 was to them of lesser importance, as long as they had willingly entered the force. Another point raised by the opponents related to the multiplicity of standards that already regulated child soldiering, and their fear that a proliferation of new treaties would increase the risk of misinterpretations (Brett, 2005; Ryle, 1999). They argued in favour of better employing international efforts to monitor compliance with existing treaties and laws, and against codifying new principles in international law, 'a body already more honoured in the breach than in the observance' (Ryle, 1999).

After several stalls in the negotiation process, an optional protocol to the Convention of the Rights of the Child on involvement of children in armed conflict was adopted in 2000 (United Nations, 2000). It called the States 'to take all feasible measures to ensure that members of their armed forces who have not yet attained the age of 18 years do not take a direct part in hostilities' (Article 3). With respect to state armies, it forbade compulsory recruitment before the age of 18 while tolerating voluntary enlistment of 16- and 17-year-olds, provided states maintain minimum safeguards to protect the minors in their ranks.[27] With respect to non-state armed groups, it unconditionally forbade recruitment under the age of 18 and criminalised the practice (Article 4).

Such 'politics of age', in Rosen's terms, has shaped the concept of childhood in international law at the expense of other reflections, by discounting the more varied and complex local understandings of children and childhood and by using age categories as instruments to advance specific agendas (Rosen, 2007). The 'straight-18' focus has ignored the fact that older teenagers are likely to differ from younger children in many ways, while infantilising 16- and 17-year-old recruits in contexts where adolescence and military life are not necessarily seen as antinomic.[28] It also focused attention on older teenagers at the expense of the younger ones, while this case study illustrates that many child recruits were in their early teens when they were recruited (which is well below the acceptable age in Côte d'Ivoire, even if we take the pragmatic view of tolerating recruitment into armed groups for the oldest teenagers).[29]

Reinsertion

In early writings, Brett and McCallin wrote something profoundly disturbing about the youngest combatants: 'These children have no skills for life in peacetime, and they are accustomed to getting their way through violence' (Brett and McCallin, 1996). Child soldiers were portrayed as having no connections in society, without skills, incompetent and prone to violence, and it was strongly implied that they were trapped in a vicious circle and that they would always experience difficulties in returning to a non-violent routine because they had been actors and witnesses of too many atrocities during the war.[30] Such a quote is disturbing because it assumes a causal relationship between processes of mobilisation and processes of demobilisation, and draws the hasty conclusion that former child recruits are cursed. Despite a lack of empirical evidence, this dramatic view has found international resonance and has often been echoed by agencies and humanitarian networks, especially when legitimising the introduction of experimental programming aiming at reinserting these children in society.

There are several debates associated with the reinsertion of child combatants. One controversy is linked to the 18 marker and the extent to which it is relevant to make a distinction between child and adult combatants using such a tool, particularly when processes of demobilisation occur within the framework of external interventions that entitle children and adults to different benefits. While much of the current debate on reinserting child soldiers is framed by the general discussion on reinserting ex-combatants – Should specific programs be created for them? Should they receive financial support to facilitate their transition to civil life? How to address stigma? – some of the approaches taken with children and adolescents are completely different from the ones taken with adults. There is for instance a wide consensus on not giving cash to child combatants in the reinsertion phase, despite the fact that this practice is increasingly widespread in adults' reinsertion processes (United Nations, 2006a). In a recent report, Human Rights Watch vehemently condemned the first attempt to give cash payments to demobilised child recruits (Human Rights Watch, 2005). The Liberian government had adopted this approach in its national DDR plan, despite several claims from UN agencies and INGOs working with children that such a policy would undermine efforts to successfully reintegrate former child soldiers into their families, and that it may make them more prone to re-recruitment. Notwithstanding this criticism, the 11,000 children who entered the Liberian DDR program between December 2003 and December 2004 were given the same allowance as adult combatants, after staying a few weeks in a transitional care centre that provided general counselling and support in searching for their families.[31] Negative effects of such safety nets included abuse and exploitation by former commanders or family members; pressure on the child to shorten his stay in the care centre to get the cash quicker (at the expense of taking the necessary time for a proper family/community reunification); and an incentive for war lords to continue recruiting children with the prospect of getting access to their share of future DDR pay-outs. Positive effects were curiously not brought forward. While it is believed, in some circles, that financial support can have positive effects on former recruits, because it can be adapted very well to fit specific individual needs at the same time as providing the necessary means to meet the immediate challenges they face (Knight and Ozerdem, 2004; Muggah, 2005; Willibald, 2006), the same reasoning rarely takes place when it comes to under-18s. With them, it is largely assumed that supplying money will bear no fruit because they are financially incompetent and easily malleable (thus prone to abuse and to diverting money from wise use). It is therefore suggested not to give any cash or to favour alternative recipients (the child's mother for instance). There are two main criticisms to this view. First, after seeing how these cash allowances were spent in Côte d'Ivoire by adult recruits – for, say: 1) reimbursing creditors, 2) responding to familial demands, 3) investing in own business, 4) allocating money to war chiefs, and 5) use for social events (such as medical expenses, home improvements) (Chelpi-den Hamer, 2009a) – one could assume that if children would receive cash allowances, they would spend them in the same ways. Second, and as seen earlier, these statements are based on a narrow view of children's development, which underestimates children's resistance to being influenced and is increasingly being questioned in academic circles.

Another wide consensus concerns specific programming and the separate treatment of children and adults. 'Children should be separated physically from adult soldiers and a security system should be established to prevent adult access to them. (…) Agencies must work together to give priority to physically removing children from contact with adult combatants' (United Nations, 2006a). This conception is based on the thought that it is possible to draw clear lines between the child and adult arenas. In practice, however, it is extremely difficult to draw such lines, as children are rarely fully disconnected from their direct environment. This case illustrated that military and post-military lives cannot be conceived as two different spaces. Many respondents never totally stopped having contact with soldiers after their demobilisation, and some continued to interact with them on a daily basis. In line with international law, international agencies have nevertheless pushed for separating

PDR activities for under-18s and for offering them other types of reinsertion packages (Williamson, 2005). One unintended consequence was that some programmes, initially designed to address the specific vulnerability of child recruits, were no longer welcomed by their end-recipients (Lee, 2009). In many settings, the youngest combatants felt betrayed and angered by the fact that they were denied access to consequent incentives and that their package differed so much from adults' reinsertion assistance. It might be quite frustrating indeed to be considered old enough to carry a Kalashnikov but to still be considered too young to receive a couple hundred dollars in cash.

Notes

1. There is currently no tangible evidence of children participating in the government's regular armed forces.
2. 3 May 2003.
3. 4 July 2003.
4. On 26 November 2005.
5. It is noteworthy that this is the first time in UN history that such an action plan has been used in matters related to child soldiering.
6. www.unicef.org/evaluation/index_49148.html
7. The four militia groups consisted of the following: FLGO, APWé, UPRGO and MILOCI.
8. The plan was similar in nature to the FAFN's and was submitted on 14 September 2006.
9. One year before, UNICEF had identified 400 children as eligible for reinsertion assistance. The list was not generated by militia leaders.
10. Although DDR had not yet started on a massive scale for the main belligerents, the dismantling of the 981 militias in the summer of 2006 followed parts of the agreed process, namely disarmament, demobilisation, receiving the financial safety net, and for half of them, entry into a pilot reinsertion project run by the German Cooperation.
11. A common argument brought by practitioners is that such centres are logistically easier to manage. It is easier to concentrate services than to manage them in dispersed areas.
12. Shepler and Stovel have both documented the political impact of defining and registering child soldiers in Sierra Leonean villages (Shepler, 2005; Stovel, 2006).
13. To date, 685 recruits from FAFN ranks and 315 militia members were officially demobilised by their commanders and entered PDR activities, along with 1000 who self-demobilised. These figures were compiled by adding the number of demobilised children presented in 2.1.
14. See appendix for the detailed interview guidelines. Most of the time, though, these guidelines were used as a checklist, and interviews took the form of a simple conversation.

15 I unfortunately could not handle them all, and I had to cancel the last interviews.
16 It included several modules to raise awareness on civic education, human rights and peace promotion.
17 30 cases out of 53 were no longer at school when the war started.
18 CM2 is the last year of the primary cycle.
19 5ème is the second year of the secondary cycle.
20 Before the war, the Ivoirian system was already characterised by a structural regional disparity in terms of enrollment rates per grade, gender divide, use of infrastructure, and completion of schooling. Formal education is the least popular in rural areas, in the northern half of the country, and among a certain fringe of the Muslim population where it competes with Quran education. The war has exacerbated existing disparities (Chelpi-den Hamer, 2007; Davies, 2004; Hugon and Bommier, 2002; Le Pape and Vidal, 1987; Proteau, 2002).
21 23 cases out of 53 were at school when the war started.
22 Rough estimates of the proportion of child soldiers forcibly recruited into armed groups come to about a third of the total (ILO 2003, in Blatmann, 2006).
23 Family support, apprenticeships, odd jobs, etc.
24 Basic equipment for setting up an independent welding workshop costs about 1,300 EUR.
25 This is in line with other studies (Honwana, 2006).
26 In international humanitarian law, a distinction is made between international and non-international armed conflicts. In international armed conflicts, 15 years is set as the minimum age for recruitment, and parties are explicitly called to refrain from recruiting children under 15 into their armed movements (Protocol I to the 1949 Geneva Conventions, Article 77). If, in exceptional cases, children under 15 take a direct part in hostilities and fall into enemy hands, the same text calls parties to continue protecting them by treating them differently than adults: 'If arrested, detained or interned for reasons related to the armed conflict, children shall be held in quarters separate from the quarters of adults, except where families are accommodated as family units.' The death penalty for an offence related to warfare does not apply to under-18s if perpetrators were so at the time the offence was committed. Non-international armed conflicts, including civil wars, are mostly regulated by the second protocol to the 1949 Geneva Conventions, especially (United Nations, 1977). With respect to child recruitment, it is reiterated that children under 15 should not be recruited into armed forces and that they deserve special protection (Article 4). It is noteworthy that the 1990 African Charter on the Rights and Welfare of the Child was the only text adopted before 2000 that did not mention 15 years as minimum age for recruitment. It defines children as 'human beings below the age of 18' and calls all parties to an armed conflict to refrain 'from recruiting any child' (Article 22). In contrast, the UN Convention on the Rights of the Child uses the same definition for

27   children but accepts the possibility of teenage recruits that are older than 15 years old (United Nations, 1989).
27 Such safeguards include: the proof that such recruitment is genuinely voluntary; informed consent of the recruit's parents or legal guardians; awareness of the duties involved in military service; the provision by the recruit of a reliable proof of age (for instance a birth certificate).
28 In many countries, in fact, it is not rare to be initiated to warfare before 18 and, at the same time, find the recruitment of 13-year-olds aberrant.
29 Respondents were between 10 and 14 years old.
30 'Many children have been physically or sexually abused by the very forces for which they have been fighting, and have seen their parents killed, sometimes in the most brutal manner, in front of their eyes. Most have also been led to participate in murder, rape and other atrocities' (Brett and McCallin, 1996).
31 The allowance was called the Transitional Safety Net (TSA) and amounted to 300 USD.

References

ATCHOARENA, D. & DELLUC, A. (2002), *Revisiting technical and vocational education in sub-Saharan Africa: An update on trends, innovations and challenges.* Paris: UNESCO/IIEP.

BETANCOURT, T. S., SINMMONS, S., BORISOVA, I., BREWER, S. E., IWEALA, U. & DE LA SOUDIERE, M. (2008), 'High Hopes, Grim Reality: Reintegration and the Education of Former Child Soldiers in Sierra Leone'. *Comparative Education Review,* 52, 565-587.

BLATMANN, C. (2006), 'The Consequences of Child Soldiering'. *HiCN Working Paper 22.* Households in Conflict Network.

BOYDEN, J. (2007), 'Children, war and world disorder in the 21st century: A review of the theories and the literature on children's contributions to armed violence'. *Conflict, Security and Development,* 7, 255-279.

BRETT, R. (2005), 'Optional Protocol to the Convention on the Rights of the Child on Involvement of Children in Armed Conflict (OP/CAC)'. *International Council on Human Rights Policy and International Commission of Jurists Workshop – Standard-setting: Lessons Learned for the Future,* Geneva.

BRETT, R. & MCCALLIN, M. (1996), *Children: The Invisible Soldiers.* Stockholm: Rädda Barnen (Save the Children Sweden).

BRETT, R. & SPECHT, I. (2004), *Young Soldiers: Why They Choose to Fight.* Boulder/London: Lynne Rienner Publishers.

CHELPI-DEN HAMER, M. (2007), 'How to certify learning in a country split into two by a civil war? Governmental and non governmental initiatives in Cote d'Ivoire, 2002-2006'. *Research in Comparative and International Education,* 2, 191-209.

CHELPI-DEN HAMER, M. (2009a), 'Reintegrating ex-combatants: what can we learn from the recent interventions in Côte d'Ivoire?' *World Conference on Humanitarian Studies,* Groningen.

CHELPI-DEN HAMER, M. (2009b), 'Why we fight? Perspectives of young combatants in western Côte d'Ivoire'. *Mobilisation for Political Violence: What do we know? – CRISE workshop,* Oxford.

DAVIES, L. (2004), *Education and Conflict: Complexity and Chaos*. London: Routledge Falmer.

DENOV, M. (2005), 'Child Soldiers in Sierra Leone: Experiences, Implications and Strategies for rehabilitation and Community Reintegration'. University of Ottawa.

DONAIS, T. (2007), *Empowerment or Imposition? Dilemmas of Local Ownership in Post-Conflict Peacebuilding Processes*, Annual meeting of the International Studies Association 48th Annual Convention, Chicago, 28 February 2007.

HART, J. (2009), 'Displaced Children's Participation in Political Violence: Towards greater understanding of mobilisation'. *CRISE Workshop on Mobilisation for Political Violence: What do we know?* Oxford.

HARVEY, R. (2000), 'Recruitment and deployment of child soldiers – The beginning of the end?' *ChildRIGHT*.

HONWANA, A. (2005), 'Innocent and Guilty: Child-Soldiers as Interstitial and Tactical Agents'. In HONWANA, A. & DE BOECK, F. (eds.) *Makers and Breakers: Children and Youth in Postcolonial Africa*. Oxford: James Currey.

HONWANA, A. (2006), *Child Soldiers in Africa*. Philadelphia: University of Pennsylvania Press.

HUGON, P. & BOMMIER, A. (2002), 'L'éducation'. In TAPINOS, G., HUGON, P., VIMARD, P. & (eds.), *La Cote d'Ivoire a l'aube du XXIe siecle – Defis demographiques et developpement durable*. Paris: Karthala.

HUMAN RIGHTS WATCH (1996), 'Children in Combat'. New York, Washington: Human Rights Watch.

HUMAN RIGHTS WATCH (2005), 'Youth, Poverty and Blood: The Lethal Legacy of West Africa's Regional Warriors'. New York: Human Rights Watch.

JENNINGS, K. M. (2007), 'The Struggle to Satisfy: DDR Through the Eyes of Ex-Combatants in Liberia'. *International Peacekeeping*, 14, 204-218.

KNIGHT, M. & OZERDEM, A. (2004), 'Guns, camps and cash: disarmament, demobilisation and reinsertion of former combatants in transition from war to peace'. *Journal of Peace Research*, 41, 499-516.

KOHLBERT, L. (1976), 'Moral Stages and Moralization: The cognitive-developmental approach'. In LICKONA, T. (ed.) *Moral development and behavior: Theory, research, and social issues*. New York: CBS College Publishing.

LE PAPE, M. & VIDAL, C. (1987), 'L'école à tout prix. Stratégies éducatives dans la petite bourgeoisie d'Abidjan'. *Actes de la recherche en sciences sociales*, 70, 64-73.

LEE, A.-J. (2009), 'Understanding and Addressing the Phenomenon of "Child Soldiers": The Gap between the Global Humanitarian Discourse and the Local Understandings and Experiences of Young People's Military Recruitment'. Refugee Studies Centre.

LONG, N. (2001), *Development Sociology – Actor perspectives.* London/New York: Routledge.
MACHEL, G. (1996), 'Impact of armed conflict on children'. United Nations.
MUGGAH, R. (2005), 'No Magic Bullet: A Critical Perspective on Disarmament, Demobilisation and Reintegration (DDR) and Weapons Reduction in Post-Conflict Contexts'. *The Round Table,* 94, 239-252.
OKETCH, M. O. (2007), 'To vocationalise or not to vocationalise? Perspectives on current trends and issues in technical and vocational education and training (TVET) in Africa'. *International Journal of Educational Development,* 27, 220-234.
PETERS, K., RICHARDS, P. & VLASSENROOT, K. (2003), 'What Happens to Youth During and After Wars? A Preliminary Review of Literature on Africa and an Assessment of the Debate'. Working paper. RAWOO.
PIAGET, J. (1972), *The Moral Judgement of the Child.* London: Routledge & Kegan Paul.
PROTEAU, L. (2002), *Passions scolaires en Cote d'Ivoire.* Paris: Karthala.
ROSEN, D. (2005), *Armies of the Young: Child soldiers in war and terrorism.* Camden: Rutgers University Press.
ROSEN, D. (2007), 'Child Soldiers, International Humanitarian Law, and the Globalisation of Childhood'. *American Anthropologist,* 109, 296-306.
RYLE, J. (1999), 'Children in Arms'. *The New York Review of Books,* 46.
SAVE THE CHILDREN (2004), 'No Place Like home? Children's experiences of reintegration in the Kailahun District of Sierra Leone'. London: Save the Children.
SAVE THE CHILDREN (2005), 'Fighting Back: Child and community-led strategies to avoid children's recruitment into armed forces and groups in West Africa'. London: Save the Children.
SHEPLER, S. (2005), 'Conflicted Childhoods: Fighting Over Child Soldiers in Sierra Leone'. Department of Social and Cultural Studies in Education, University of California Berkeley.
SINGER, P. W. (2006), *Children at War.* Berkeley and Los Angeles: University of California Press.
STOVEL, L. (2006), 'Long road home: Building reconciliation and trust in postwar Sierra Leone'. Department of Sociology and Anthropology, Simon Fraser University.
UNITED NATIONS (1977), Protocol II Additional to the Geneva Conventions of 12 August 1949, and Relating to the Protection of Victims of Non-International Armed Conflicts.
UNITED NATIONS (1989), Convention on the Rights of the Child. United Nations/Office of the High Commissioner for Human Rights.

UNITED NATIONS (2000), Optional Protocol to the Convention on the Rights of the Child on the involvement of children in armed conflicts.

UNITED NATIONS (2005), Report of the Secretary-General on children and armed conflict. United Nations Security Council.

UNITED NATIONS (2006a), 'Integrated Disarmament, Demobilisation and Reintegration Standards – Children and DDR'. UN DPKO.

UNITED NATIONS (2006b), Report of the Secretary-General on children and armed conflict in Cote d'Ivoire. United Nations Security Council.

UNITED NATIONS (2007), Report of the Secretary-General on children and armed conflict in Cote d'Ivoire. United Nations Security Council.

WILLIAMSON, J. (2005), 'Reintegration of Child Soldiers in Sierra Leone'. Washington D.C.: DCOF/USAID.

WILLIBALD, S. (2006), 'Does money work? Cash transfers to ex-combatants in disarmament and reintegration processes'. *Disasters*, 30, 316-339.

APPENDIX: Interview Guide (in French) - Checklist

1   **Informations générales**

Nom de l'enfant: _____

Sexe: ☐ Homme   ☐ Femme

Groupe ethnique: _____

Religion: _____

Age (actuel): _____

Lieu de naissance de l'enfant: _____

Nom du père: _____

Profession du père: _____

Père décédé?   ☐ Oui – Préciser l'année: _   ☐ Non

Nom de la mère: _____

Profession de la mère: _____

Mère décédée?   ☐ Oui – Préciser l'année: _   ☐ Non

Parents divorcés?   ☐ Oui – Préciser l'année: _   ☐ Non

Nbre de frères et sœurs (biologiques), leur âge, leur lieu de résidence: ___

	Age (actuel)	Lieu de résidence	Avec qui habitent-ils?
Frère 1			
Frère 2			
Frère 3			
Frère 4			

	Age (actuel)	Lieu de résidence	Avec qui habitent-ils?
Sœur 1			
Sœur 2			
Sœur 3			
Sœur 4			

Position de l'enfant dans la fratrie:

☐ Aîné de famille   ☐ 1er fils   ☐ Autres _____

2 **Avant son recrutement dans les forces armées**

Lieu de résidence de l'enfant: _____

Avec qui habitait-t-il?

☐ avec ses deux parents biologiques

☐ avec seulement un de ses parents biologiques (son père ou sa mère)

☐ avec un tuteur qui est un membre de sa famille
  – Préciser qui: _____

☐ avec un tuteur qui n'est pas un membre de sa famille (sans lien de parenté)
  – Préciser qui: _____

☐ Seul

Profession de la personne chez qui l'enfant habitait: _____

Avant la guerre, qui payait ses dépenses d'habits?

☐ ses deux parents biologiques

☐ seulement un de ses parents biologiques (son père ou sa mère)
  – Préciser: _____

☐ un tuteur qui est un membre de sa famille
  – Préciser qui: _____

☐ un tuteur qui n'est pas un membre de sa famille (sans lien de parenté)
  – Préciser qui: _____
☐ l'enfant se débrouillait lui-même, en travaillant

Avant la guerre, qui payait sa nourriture?
☐ ses deux parents biologiques
☐ seulement un de ses parents biologiques (son père ou sa mère)
  – Préciser: _____
☐ un tuteur qui est un membre de sa famille
  – Préciser qui: _____
☐ un tuteur qui n'est pas un membre de sa famille (sans lien de parenté)
  – Préciser qui: _____
☐ l'enfant se débrouillait lui-même, en travaillant

Parcours scolaire de l'enfant

L'enfant sait-il lire?	☐ Oui	☐ Non
L'enfant sait-il écrire?	☐ Oui	☐ Non
L'enfant sait-il compter?	☐ Oui	☐ Non
L'enfant est-il allé à l'école primaire?	☐ Oui	☐ Non
Est-il allé à l'école secondaire?	☐ Oui	☐ Non

Faire la liste des écoles primaires et secondaires que l'enfant a fréquentées (en précisant: nom des écoles, nom des villages ou villes, de quelle classe à quelle classe, avec qui habitait l'enfant):

_____

_____

L'enfant a-t-il été boursier?   ☐ Oui   ☐ Non

Dernière classe fréquentée (préciser l'année):

_____

Pourquoi l'enfant a-t-il arrêté de fréquenter l'école?

☐ par manque de moyens de ses parents / de son tuteur

☐ à cause de la guerre, les écoles ont fermé

☐ par perte d'intérêt pour les études

☐ pour se mettre à travailler à plein temps

☐ Autres

— Préciser: _____

Durant sa scolarité, l'enfant a-t-il redoublé?

☐ —Oui

— Préciser quelles classes: _____

☐ —Non

Est-il allé à l'école coranique? ☐ Oui ☐ Non

Pendant combien de temps: _____

Où: _____

Est-il allé dans une école privée? ☐ Oui ☐ Non

Pendant combien de temps: _____

Où: _____

Au cours de sa scolarité, qui payait les fournitures scolaires de l'enfant?

☐ ses deux parents biologiques

☐ seulement un de ses parents biologiques (son père ou sa mère)

— Préciser: _____

☐ un tuteur qui est un membre de sa famille

— Préciser qui: _____

☐ un tuteur qui n'est pas un membre de sa famille (sans lien de parenté)

— Préciser qui: _____

☐ l'enfant se débrouillait lui-même, en travaillant

Au cours de sa scolarité, qui payait ses dépenses d'habits?

☐ ses deux parents biologiques

☐ seulement un de ses parents biologiques (son père ou sa mère)
   – Préciser: _____

☐ un tuteur qui est un membre de sa famille
   – Préciser qui: _____

☐ un tuteur qui n'est pas un membre de sa famille (sans lien de parenté)
   – Préciser qui: _____

☐ l'enfant se débrouillait lui-même, en travaillant

Au cours de sa scolarité, qui payait sa nourriture?

☐ ses deux parents biologiques

☐ seulement un de ses parents biologiques (son père ou sa mère)
   – Préciser: _____

☐ un tuteur qui est un membre de sa famille
   – Préciser qui: _____

☐ un tuteur qui n'est pas un membre de sa famille (sans lien de parenté)
   – Préciser qui: _____

☐ l'enfant se débrouillait lui-même, en travaillant

Activités

Dans quelles activités l'enfant était-il impliqué avant la guerre?

☐ travaux champêtres (aide à la famille dans le champ familial)

☐ travaux champêtres (l'enfant était employé comme manœuvre dans d'autres champs pour gagner un peu d'argent)

☐ en apprentissage chez un parent pendant les vacances
   – Préciser quelle activité: _____

- ☐ pousseur de brouette
- ☐ petits contrats
  - Préciser pour quel type de travail: _____
- ☐ petit commerce
  - Préciser quoi: _____
- ☐ Autres activités
  - Préciser quoi: _____
- ☐ Rien

Si l'enfant gagnait un peu d'argent, que faisait-il avec?

- ☐ Il donnait tout aux parents
- ☐ Il donnait une partie seulement aux parents, le reste, pour lui
- ☐ Il gardait tout pour lui

Relations avec la famille

Y avait-t-il une bonne entente entre l'enfant et son père (si non ou sans contact, précisez pourquoi)? _____

Y avait-t-il une bonne entente entre l'enfant et sa mère? _____

Y avait-t-il une bonne entente entre l'enfant et sa marâtre? _____

Y avait-t-il une bonne entente entre l'enfant et son beau-père? _____

Y avait-t-il une bonne entente entre l'enfant et les autres membres de sa famille? _____

Y avait-t-il une bonne entente entre l'enfant et son entourage? _____

L'enfant a-t-il déjà été en conflit avec un membre de sa famille? Si oui pour quelles raisons? _____

L'enfant a-t-il déjà été en conflit avec son entourage? Si oui pour quelles raisons? _____

3   Dans les forces armées

L'enfant connaissait-il quelqu'un dans les forces armées avant de prendre les armes?

☐ Oui, un membre de sa famille
   – Préciser qui: _____

☐ Oui, un ami
   – Préciser qui: _____

☐ Oui, une connaissance
   – Préciser qui: _____

☐ Non, l'enfant ne connaissait personne avant de rejoindre les forces armées.

Pourquoi l'enfant a-t-il rejoint les forces armées?

☐ Parce qu'on lui a fait des promesses
   – Préciser quoi: _____

☐ Pour gagner de l'argent

☐ Pour protéger sa famille

☐ Pour se venger

☐ L'enfant a été pris de force

☐ Les parents l'ont encouragé   ☐ Autres: _____

Liste des camps militaires où l'enfant a été affecté en commençant par le lieu de recrutement jusqu'au lieu de démobilisation:

	Nom du camp	Ville/Village	De quand à quand
Camp 1, 2, 3…			De: _____ A: _____

Où dormait-il le plus souvent?

☐ au camp militaire

☐ chez des amis militaires

☐ chez un tuteur militaire

☐ chez des amis civils

☐ dehors

☐ seul

☐ chez ses deux parents biologiques

☐ chez un de ses deux parents biologiques

☐ chez un tuteur (lien familial)

– Préciser qui: _____

☐ chez un tuteur (sans lien familial)

– Préciser qui: _____

Retournait-il fréquemment dans sa famille, en permission?

Dans quelles activités l'enfant était-il impliqué? (plusieurs réponses possibles)

☐ garde au corridor (barrage)

☐ garde des prisonniers

☐ petites courses pour les militaires

☐ travaux ménagers au camp

☐ combattant

☐ garde du corps

☐ Autres

– Précisez quoi: _____

L'enfant a-t-il subi des violences physiques au camp? ☐ Oui ☐ Non

Raisons de sortie de l'armée?

- ☐ démobilisation officielle (par le chef de caserne et avec un papier officiel)
- ☐ démobilisation non officielle (par le chef de caserne ou des militaires, sans papier officiel)
- ☐ l'enfant s'est auto-démobilisé:
    - ☐ l'enfant est parti en permission et n'est pas revenu
    - ☐ un parent de l'enfant a pu négocier son départ avec les militaires
    - ☐ l'enfant a fui
    - ☐ Autres: _____

4   Démobilisation – Retour à la vie civile

Lieu de résidence actuel de l'enfant: _____

Avec qui habite-t-il?

- ☐ avec ses deux parents biologiques
- ☐ avec seulement un de ses parents biologiques (son père ou sa mère)
- ☐ avec son patron (d'apprentissage)
- ☐ avec un tuteur qui est un membre de sa famille
    - Préciser qui: _____
- ☐ avec un tuteur qui n'est pas un membre de sa famille (sans lien de parente)
    - Préciser qui: _____
- ☐ Seul
- ☐ Avec des amis

Profession de la personne chez qui l'enfant habite:

_____

Contact téléphonique de la personne chez qui il habite:
_____

Y a-t-il une bonne entente entre l'enfant et la personne chez qui il habite?
☐ Oui   ☐ Non

L'enfant est-il inscrit à l'école en ce moment?
☐ Oui   ☐ Non

En quelle classe? _____

Suit-il une formation d'apprentissage?
☐ Oui   ☐ Non

Quelle activité?   ☐ Couture   ☐ Mécanique auto   ☐ Mécanique moto
☐ Menuiserie   ☐ Electricité/Plomberie   ☐ Informatique

☐ Autres – Préciser: _____

Y a-t-il une bonne entente entre l'enfant et son patron?
☐ Oui   ☐ Non

Y a-t-il une bonne entente entre l'enfant et les autres collègues?
☐ Oui   ☐ Non

Y a-t-il suffisamment de clients à l'atelier?
☐ Oui   ☐ Non

L'enfant souhaiterait-t-il continuer son apprentissage chez le même patron et dans la même activité?
☐ Oui   ☐ Non

Retourne-il fréquemment dans sa famille?
☐ Oui   ☐ Non

Y a-t-il une bonne entente entre l'enfant et sa famille?

☐ Oui ☐ Non

Où l'enfant veut-il continuer à habiter dans le futur?

☐ au village ☐ en ville ☐ les 2, au village et en ville
☐ seul ☐ en famille

Qui paye désormais ses dépenses d'habits et sa nourriture?

☐ l'enfant se débrouille lui-même, en travaillant

☐ ses deux parents biologiques

☐ seulement un de ses parents biologiques (son père ou sa mère)
   – Préciser: _____

☐ un tuteur qui est un membre de sa famille
   – Préciser qui: _____

☐ un tuteur qui n'est pas un membre de sa famille (sans lien de parente)
   – Préciser qui: _____

Printed in Germany
by Amazon Distribution
GmbH, Leipzig